INFORMATION TECHNOLOGY FOR BUSINESS USERS

A guide to the Information Technology jargon

Short, simple, and to-the-point explanation of IT jargon with illustrations. Helpful for non-technical business users to make more informed decisions while working with technical teams.

Manu Agrawal (MBA, MCITP, MCTS)
www.HelloManu.com

TABLE OF CONTENTS

Smart Industry (Industry 4.0)

Robotics

Hyperautomation

Thank you for reading

INTRODUCTION

Having worked in Information Technology, I can't help but notice the communication gap that exists between the business and the IT teams. In the context of Information Technology, Sigmund Freud's words *"If youth knew; if age could"* could be translated as *"If developers knew; if business could"*.

Developers who understand business better; and Business folks who understand technology better are at an advantage while communicating with colleagues or co-founders or making informed decisions.

This book aims to explain daily technical jargon in really a simple language without any pep talk or overly long descriptions, mostly in one or two simple sentences with examples from daily life.

Feedback is welcome so I can improve my future work.

Without further ado, let's dive right in.

ARTIFICIAL INTELLIGENCE (AI)

A system that can **learn, discriminate** and **predict**, somewhat like human brain.

E.g. Autocorrect spelling and grammar in MS Word, Self-driving cars, Google Images that can discriminate plants from trees or from cars.

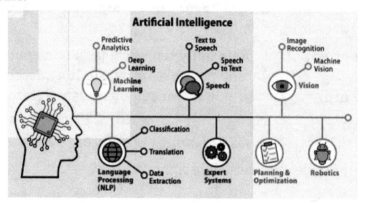

MACHINE LEARNING (ML)

Machine learning utilizes artificial intelligence to enable a system to naturally upgrade on its own, without any outside help.

E.g. a software that learns to extract features in a picture and recognize if it is a car or not.

Machine Learning

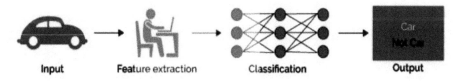

Input   Feature extraction   Classification   Output

DEEP LEARNING

This is a function of Artificial Intelligence (AI) that emulates the human brain's workings in processing data and creating patterns for decision-making or predicting.

E.g. a computer program that learns to recognize cars in a picture.

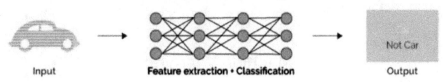

Deep Learning

| Input | Feature extraction • Classification | Output |

NEURAL NETWORK

A chunk of programming code that tries to perceive fundamental connections in given data, just like a human brain will do. In this sense, neural networks refer to frameworks of neurons, either natural or artificial.

E.g. Handwriting recognition applications, Image recognition applications like Google Images. Or a software that can accept weight and height as input and try to predict the gender of a person.

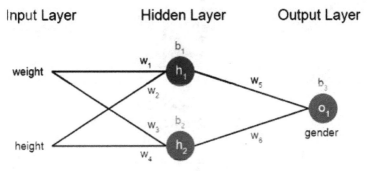

THE INTERNET OF THINGS (IOT)

The Internet of Things (IoT) is an arrangement of interrelated, internet-connected items that can gather and transfer data over a remote network without human mediation.

E.g. Refrigerator that can order milk when milk has run out. Or issue a flood warning when water level in a river reaches a critical threshold.

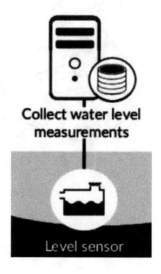

SOFTWARE AS A SERVICE (SAAS)

Software as a Service (SaaS) is a software licensing model in which access to the software is leased. The software is placed on cloud/external servers rather than on servers situated in-house of the buyer.

E.g. Gmail, Box, Dropbox.

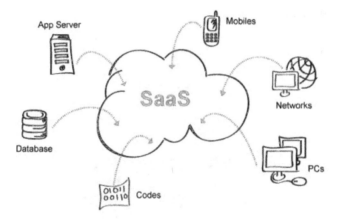

PLATFORM AS A SERVICE (PAAS)

Also known as Application Platform as a Service (aPaaS) is a cloud services where developers can host and manage their applications remotely.

E.g. Google App Engine, Windows Azure, AWS Lambada.

The diagram below represents the relationship between SaaS, Paas/aPaas, and Iaas.

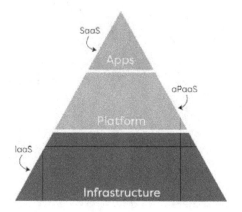

CAAS (CONTAINER AS A SERVICE)

CaaS is a cloud service that allows software developers to organize, execute, manage, scale and stop containers as needed.

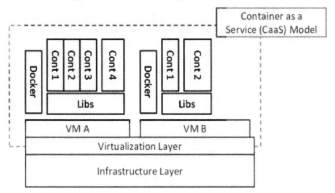

THE INTERNET OF BEHAVIORS (IOB)

IoB is study and utilization of behaviors of people while online. This includes social networking, self-representation, pro, and anti-social behaviors (e.g., disinhibition & cyberbullying).

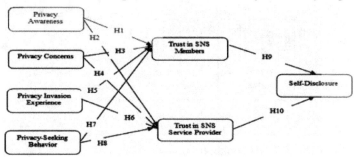

INFRASTRUCTURE AS A SERVICE (IAAS)

Infrastructure as a service (IaaS) is a cloud service used to provision and manage infrastructure via code, over the cloud.

It is one of the four kinds of cloud services, along with software as a service (SaaS), platform as a service (PaaS), and functions as a service (FAAS).

E.g. Amazon Web Services (AWS), Azure, Digital Ocean

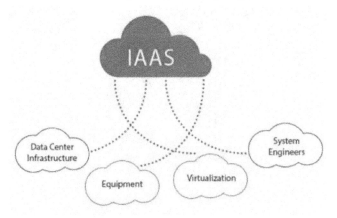

AUGMENTED REALITY (AR)

Augmented reality augments or enhances the real world experiences. Enhancement can be for any experience like visual, audio, touch, smell etc.

E.g. Haptic feedback on your fingers while typing on mobile keyboard

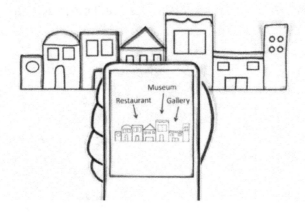

VIRTUAL REALITY (VR)

Virtual reality (VR) is a computer-generated simulation of a real experience. An individual can interact inside an artificial three-dimensional environment utilizing electronic gadgets.

E.g. VR Glasses or VR Kits, 6-D movies in theme parks like Universal Studios

EXTENDED REALITY (XR)

Extended reality (XR) is a term alluding to all real-and-virtual collaborative environments and human-machine interactions initiated by computer technology with wearables. The 'X' is just a variable for any current or future spatial figuring advances.

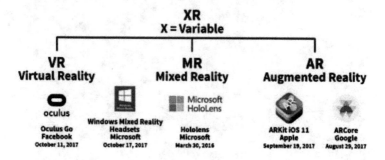

CRYPTOCURRENCY

A cryptocurrency uses encrypted computer files as cash. Cryptocurrencies use 'decentralized control,' which means that they aren't controlled by one person or the government.

Example: Bitcoin

Cryptocurrency is an encrypted string of data or a hash, encoded to signify one unit of currency.

BITCOIN

A form of digital currency on which a record of transactions is maintained.

If you can solve computer based mathematical challenges then you can generate or mint bitcoins. The complexity of the challenge keep increasing. In early days even laptops could solve those challenges, but now in 2020 it needs very powerful specialized software.

BLOCK CHAIN

Block chain refers to a digital record of negotiations. The term originates from its structure, in which individual records, called blocks, are connected as a chain.

E.g. Bitcoins, Crypto currencies are based on block chain technology

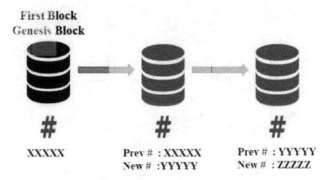

BLOCKS CANNOT BE MODIFIED OR DELETED

DATA SCIENCE

Data science is the subject field that merges domain mastery, programming aptitudes, and information on mathematics and statistics to extract meaningful data understanding.

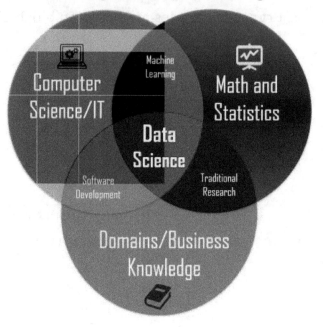

DATA MINING

Data mining is used to extract usable data from any raw data e.g. from websites or text files etc.. It analyzes data patterns in large batches of data and extracts only the required pieces. Data mining is also known as Knowledge Discovery in Data (KDD).

E.g. a computer app or script can scan the web pages of Facebook profiles and make a database of people. It will be against Facebook policies though.

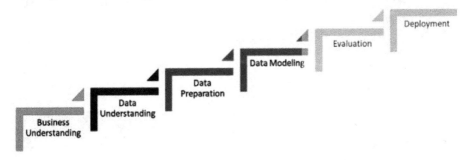

BIG DATA

As the name suggests, it is a very large set of data (which is being generated at a very fast speed), that is too varied and too complex to deal with traditional strategies.

E.g. Worldwide total of Facebook messages, E-mails sent on Gmail

DEVOPS

DevOps takes its name from Development (Dev) and Operations (Ops). It is the philosophy or practices where Development and Operations go hand in hand and not in a sequential manner.

Planning, coding, testing, monitoring, deployment, operations all happen in tandem with each other simultaneously.

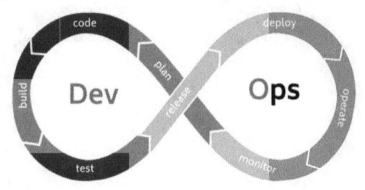

CI/CD

Continuous integration (CI) and continuous delivery (CD) typify a culture, set of operating principles, and collection of practices that enable application advancement teams to deliver code changes more much of the time and reliably. This utilization is also known as the CI/CD pipeline.

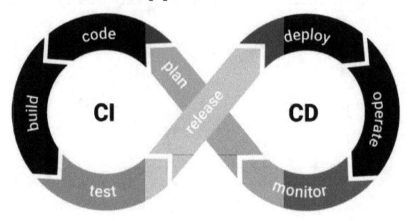

AGILE

A philosophy of product development to create working pieces in short timeframes. Planned in a cyclical timetable of progress, production, and distribution.

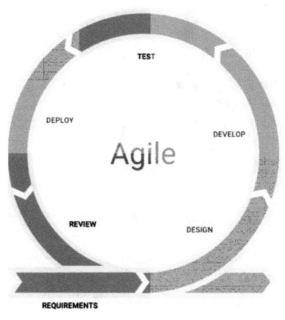

SCRUM

Scrum is a framework that implements the principles of Agile as a concrete set of artefacts, practices, and roles.

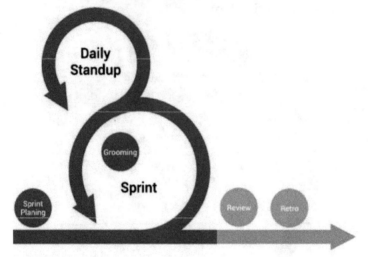

CLOUD COMPUTING

Cloud computing is the on-demand availability of computer resources, like storage space and computing power. These resources are managed by the provider and not by the user.

E.g. Gmail is hosted on Google's cloud. Netflix movies are on cloud

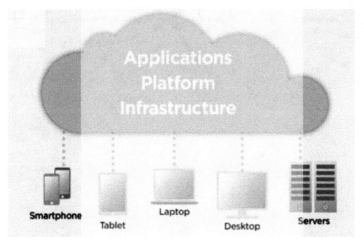

DISTRIBUTED CLOUD

A distributed cloud has geographically distributed infrastructure. With a distributed cloud model, organizations decrease latency, network congestion, and the danger of data loss.

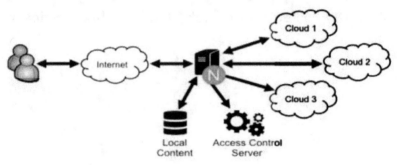

CDN

CDN (Content Delivery Network) providers cache data or content across their servers worldwide.

E.g. Users from all over the world connect to a website that has copies stored on CDN providers' servers all over the world. The users automatically request data/content from the closest location to reduce details and increase speed. E.g. California users get served by servers in West Coast.

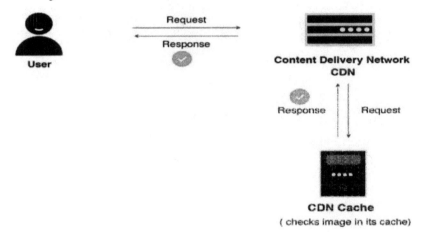

NODE

Any system or device connected to a network is referred as a node.

E.g. Computer, mobile, laptop, server, printer, virtual machine, container, Internet connected devices like washing machines, smart TVs etc.

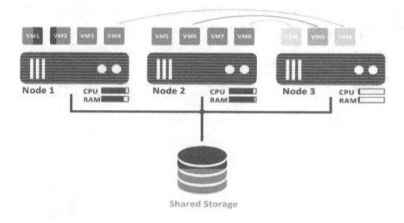

VIRTUAL MACHINE (VM)

A virtual computer system made from virtualizing the hardware of a real computer called the host. A VM utilizes CPU, memory, network interface, and storage, of the host computer. One host computer can have several VMs.

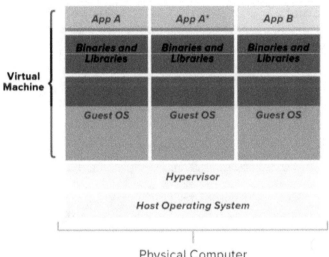

CONTAINERS

A Container is a separation inside a host operating system (OS) to isolate a software application, data, etc. Containers virtualize the OS so several Containers can use the same OS host.

Containers are lightweight as they do not contain OS image (unlike VMs).

Container managers like Kubernetes or Docker Swarm can manage Containers.

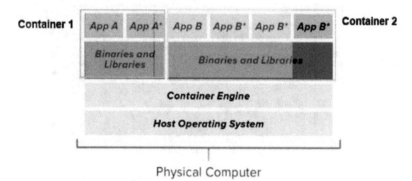

Physical Computer

KUBERNETES (K8S)

Kubernetes (commonly known as "K8s") is an open-source system that can manage Containers or Container Clusters. It can deploy or scale Containers on demand as per configuration.

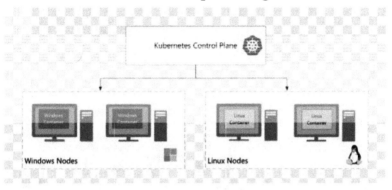

DOCKER SWARM

A Docker Swarm is a cluster of physical or virtual machines running the Docker application. Most developers tend to prefer Kubernetes over Docker Swarm.

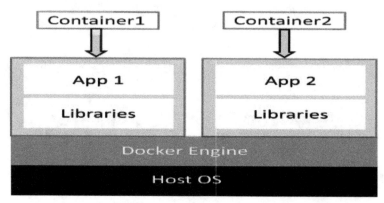

QUANTUM COMPUTING

In Standard computers that we use, information can be stored in two bits which can have only one of four possible states (00, 01, 10, or 11). Quantum computers on the other hand, use qubits, which can have all four possible states at the same time.

A regular computer tries to solve a problem by trying things sequentially, one by one until it finds a solution. But a quantum computer can try all or several paths at once – in essence, finding a solution much faster.

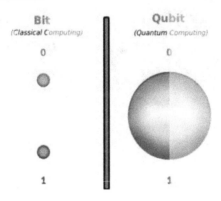

SMART INDUSTRY (INDUSTRY 4.0)

Completely integrated, collaborative manufacturing systems that react realistically to satisfy changing needs and conditions in the intelligent factory, inventory network, and client needs.

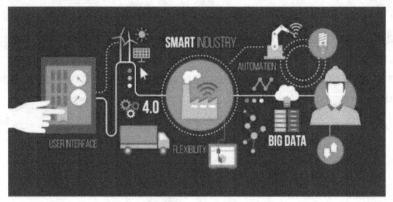

ROBOTICS

Robotics is design, construction, and implementation of machines (robots) to do specific functions.

E.g. Agricultural Robots, Automatic vacuum cleaners

HYPERAUTOMATION

Hyperautomation augments workers and automates processes in ways that are a lot more impactful that traditional automation. It uses RPA (Robotic Process Automation), Artificial Intelligence, Machine Learning and extraction process

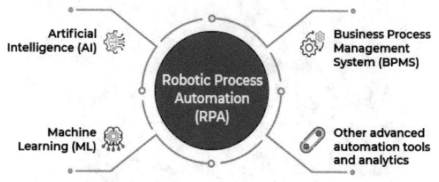

THANK YOU FOR READING

Your taking time to read this is appreciated. Please feel free to contact the author by visiting www.HelloManu.com and leave your feedback which can be helpful for future work.